ASTOUNDING
MUSHROOMS

A Firefly Book

Published by Firefly Books Ltd. 2022

First printing

Library of Congress Control Number: 2022933495

Library and Archives Canada Cataloguing in Publication
Title: Astounding mushrooms / photographs by
   Jaroslav Malý with text by Alain Bellocq.
Other titles: Étonnants champignons. English
Names: Malý, Jaroslav, photographer. | Bellocq, Alain, 1943- author.
Description: Translation of: Étonnants champignons. | Previously
   published: Richmond Hill, Ontario: Firefly Books, 2015.
Identifiers: Canadiana 20220179344 | ISBN 9780228103868 (softcover)
Subjects: LCSH: Mushrooms—Identification. | LCSH: Mushrooms—Pictorial works.
Classification: LCC QK617 .M3813 2022 | DDC 579.6022/2—dc23

Published in the United States by
Firefly Books (U.S.) Inc.
P.O. Box 1338, Ellicott Station
Buffalo, New York 14205

Published in Canada by
Firefly Books Ltd.
50 Staples Avenue, Unit 1
Richmond Hill, Ontario L4B 0A7

Printed in China

Important Poisoning Disclaimer

The content in this book is for information and interest only. It is not an identification guide to mushrooms and fungi and it should not be interpreted as such. Firefly Books Ltd., its distributors and all other parties with which it has any business, personal or otherwise, accepts no liability for any injury or death occurring as a result of ingesting or exposure to any mushroom or fungi described or listed in this book. Many mushrooms are poisonous and some are deadly poisonous. We have made every effort to ensure accuracy but the responsibility for eating any mushroom or fungus rests solely with the individual, including any outcome due to allergy or intolerance for any mushroom or fungus, whatever the species. If you collect any mushrooms to eat, make sure that your identification checks out in every detail. **Never eat any wild mushroom until an expert mycologist has checked your identification.** Even when you know a mushroom well, weather conditions or animal damage can cause differences in appearance that could lead to misidentification.

Note: Reference to "Europe" includes the European continent and the United Kingdom of Great Britain and Northern Ireland.

Conceived by Éditions Glénat
Couvent Sainte-Cécile
37, rue Servan
38000 Grenoble

ASTOUNDING
MUSHROOMS

Photographs by **Jaroslav Malý**
with text by **Alain Bellocq**

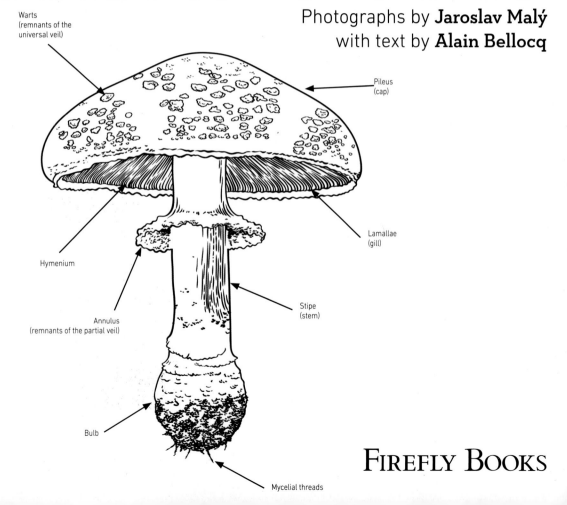

Warts
(remnants of the
universal veil)

Pileus
(cap)

Hymenium

Lamallae
(gill)

Annulus
(remnants of the partial veil)

Stipe
(stem)

Bulb

Mycelial threads

FIREFLY BOOKS

Contents

As its surroundings here make clear, the Clouded Funnel or Clouded Agaric (*Clitocybe nebularis*) is a late species. Although it can sometimes be poisonous, it is widely eaten, especially in eastern France.

The Fungus Kingdom

Neither plants nor animals, fungi constitute what specialists call Mycota, or the fungus kingdom. On the tree of life, fungi are closer to animals than to plants. Indeed, fungi have many traits in common with animals, including the inability to perform photosynthesis, because they lack chlorophyll in their cells. Fungi must therefore obtain the organic material that they need to grow from other organisms; in scientific terms, they are heterotrophic. Another trait that fungi share with animals is that they store carbohydrates in the form of glycogen, whereas plants do so in the form of starch. Fungi even produce chitin, a nitrogen-containing substance that forms their cell walls and that is also found in the exoskeletons of insects.

The fungus kingdom includes all organisms that meet the following criteria. They must have a nucleus in each cell (which defines them as eukaryotes), cell walls made of chitin, and a vegetative apparatus (mycelium) composed of a network of microscopic filaments called hyphae. To be considered fungi, organisms must also reproduce by spores and be heterotrophic and absorbotrophic (digest their nutrients outside their cells, then absorb them in the form of small molecules through their cell walls).

Although the number of fungus species is not known, fungi are probably the most numerous living organisms after insects. About 100,000 species of fungi have been described so far worldwide, but the total number in existence is estimated at 1 to 1.5 million. Many new species are being discovered every year, and the task of inventorying them all is far from over.

An Ancient Realm

Very little is known about the origins of fungi, and fossil fungi are unfortunately extremely scarce. Some rare specimens have been found preserved in amber, including a *Coprinites dominicana* (an extinct species closely related to the genus *Coprinus*) discovered in the Dominican Republic and dated at over 15 million years old. The oldest mushroom fossils ever found date back more than 400 million years, to the Devonian period, when the first terrestrial vertebrates appeared. Among these fossils are some Chytridiomycota — also known as chytrids — the most primitive fungi still living on Earth. The chytrids are microscopic species. They are mostly aquatic, and their spores have the distinctive feature of a flagellum that gives them mobility.

Many mushrooms grow in the woods, including many species of *Pholiota*, such as the Shaggy Scalycap (*Pholiota squarrosa*) shown here.

What Are Mushrooms?

But what exactly are mushrooms? Like a plant, a fungus consists of a vegetative portion and a reproductive portion. In fungi, the vegetative portion is the mycelium, and the reproductive portion is the sporophore. This sporophore is what we usually call a "mushroom." In this book, we will be talking only about macroscopic fungi: those whose sporophore is visible to the naked eye.

The mycelium of a fungus usually grows underground, and it grows constantly, to a considerable size and age. The world record is currently held by an *Armillaria ostoyae* in Oregon, in the United States. This living fungus is over 2,400 years old. Its mycelium weighs around 661 tons (600 tonnes) and covers an area of nearly 3.5 square miles (9 km²)!

In contrast, the sporophore of a fungus lives a much shorter time: scarcely a few hours, in the case of certain coprinoid fungi; sometimes just a few day; and a few years at most for certain polypores, such as the tinder fungus. The sporophore is usually aerial, but in some species, such as truffles, it grows underground. In some cases it is tiny, measuring a few thousandths of an inch at most, but in others, it can reach impressive dimensions. For example, the Giant Puffball can weigh over 22 pounds (10 kg) and exceed 27 inches (70 cm). Mushrooms vary tremendously in appearance, which is why it is always so exciting and amazing to see them grow.

Feeding and Reproducing

Fungi feed in three different ways. One large group of fungi, known as saprophytes, feed on decomposing organic matter. A smaller group, parasitic fungi, feed on other living organisms. The third group comprises numerous fungi that maintain symbiotic relationships with other living organisms: either plants or animals. (Fungi that live in symbiosis with vascular plants are known as mycorrhizal fungi.)

The sole function of the sporophore (the mushroom) is to produce and spread spores, which then germinate and develop into a new, primary mycelium. But whereas in plants, a single seed develops into an entire new plant, in fungi, two primary mycelia must merge to create a secondary mycelium, and only the secondary mycelium can produce new sporophores. Note, however, that some fungi can also propagate vegetatively, a form of asexual reproduction that results in the birth of clones.

Armillaria species are widely eaten in Germany and should preferably be gathered when young. This Dark Honey Fungus (*Armillaria ostoyae*) has a white ring and can be recognized by its dark cap.

Mushrooms and Humankind

People use mushrooms in many different ways. The most widespread use, of course, is as food. Mushrooms were a prized delicacy in Ancient Rome and were first cultivated in Asia over 900 years ago. Nowadays, hundreds of thousands of mushroom lovers go hunting for them in the fall, even though many mushroom species can be poisonous or even fatal to eat.

Mushrooms can also have medicinal properties, as was already known in prehistoric times – for example, traces of three species of medicinal mushrooms were found in the equipment of Ötzi the Iceman, the Neolithic hunter whose naturally mummified body was found frozen in the ice in the Austro-Italian Alps in 1991. Today, more and more research is being done on the medicinal properties of mushrooms, with some promising results.

The use of mushrooms for ritual, spiritual and religious purposes also dates back to the dawn of time. Even now, shamans in some cultures still use hallucinogenic mushrooms, which the Aztecs worshipped as the "flesh of the gods," to enter into the invisible world.

But you don't need to eat magic mushrooms to share in the magic of the mushroom world. In their effort to produce as many spores as possible and spread them as effectively as possible, mushrooms grow in such a variety of sizes, shapes and colors, and have so many different smells and textures, that you can experience their magic with your ordinary senses alone. Simply go outside and walk around with your eyes open for mushrooms large and small. We hope that the beautiful photographs on the following pages will inspire you to do just that!

Swamp Beacons (*Mitrula paludosa*) are found only in flooded ditches or wetland soils where there is standing or moving water.

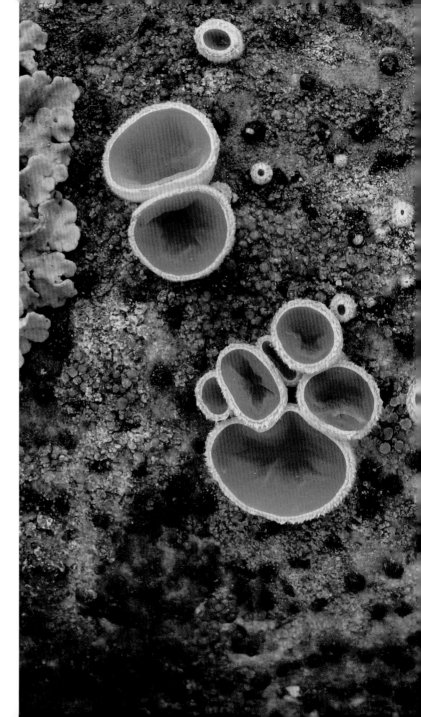

Poplar Bells (*Schizophyllum amplum*) look something like the Judas's Ear or certain cup fungi, but their fertile surface (the hymenium) faces downward.

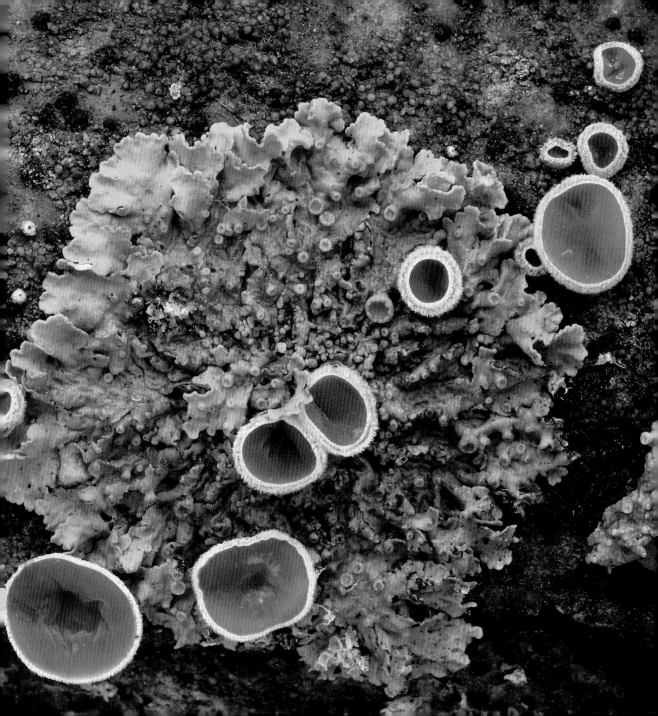

Veiled Mushrooms

In many species of fungi, the immature mushroom is surrounded by a protective membrane called the universal veil, which eventually breaks open to let the mushroom emerge. This veil is very apparent in *Amanita* and *Volvariella* mushrooms. Universal veils vary widely in their thickness and toughness, so they are ruptured or broken down in a variety of ways. In some species, the consistency of this veil varies from one portion to another. At one extreme, the veil may be highly tenacious, cracking open like an egg and leaving a very tough, cuplike volva at the base of the stem, but no warts or patches on the cap. At the other extreme, the veil may be very brittle, especially at its base; as the cap emerges, it shatters the veil and carries most of the remnants along with it, so that they form numerous scaly patches on its surface. In some cases, the universal veil is elongated into an armilla that surrounds the stem like a sock and may have a ring at the top.

The hymenium (fertile surface) in many gilled mushrooms and some tubed mushrooms is protected by a partial veil, or secondary veil. As the cap develops, the veil comes detached from it and may collapse around the stem to form a ring. This ring may be merely a faint trace of the original veil or may be quite pronounced, and it varies in form from one species to another (for example, it may be hanging, flaring, or sheathlike). In some gilled mushrooms, in particular cortinars, the partial veil is a network of thin threads resembling a spiderweb and known as the cortina. This cortina is quite visible on the immature mushroom but soon falls away onto the stem.

Caesar's Mushroom (*Amanita caesarea*) is one of the most highly prized edible mushrooms. The remnants of the membranous veil from which this young specimen emerged is seen in the white, relatively thick volva around the base of its stem.

This Tawny Grisette (*Amanita fulva*) has just broken through the veil that encased it. The ochraceous volva is still visible in the adult specimen to the right.

Above

The ring left behind by the partial veil is clearly apparent on the stem of this Pearly Powdercap (*Cystoderma carcharias*).

Left

The Piggyback Rosegill (*Volvaria surrecta*) grows, often in groups, on decomposing Clouded Funnel Cap mushrooms (*Clitocybe nebularis*). It has a whitish, very fibrous cap, but even more distinctive is the white, membranous volva (cup) at its base.

Above

The Blusher (*Amanita rubescens*) is poisonous when eaten raw. This species is very common in coniferous and deciduous woodlands in summer and fall. It is characterized by wine-colored reddening where bruised or damaged, especially at the base of the stem. Its cap ranges from reddish brown to almost white and is covered with dark, scaly patches.

Right

The Royal Fly Agaric (*Amanita regalis*) closely resembles the Fly Agaric (*Amanita muscaria*) but has a cap tending more toward brown and yellowing with age. It is more common in northern Europe. Specimens with as many warts on their caps as this one are rare.

Above

The Gray Veiled Amanita (*Amanita porphyria*) has a lovely purple-brown cap and a skirtlike ring that soon turns violet-gray. It grows mainly on conifers.

Right

The False Deathcap (*Amanita citrina*) gives off a strong odor of rapeseed or raw potato. The base of the stem is a marginate bulb with a distinct rim. This species is no longer considered deadly, but it does have an unpleasant taste.

Preceding two-page spread, left

On these young specimens of the Funeral Bell (*Galerina marginata*), the hymenium is still covered by the secondary veil, which will leave a ring when it falls away. This small but potentially deadly mushroom is fairly common in woodlands and on mosses.

Preceding two-page spread, right

The Bulbous Honey Fungus (*Armillaria gallica*) can be recognized by its white, yellow-edged armilla. On these young specimens, the ring is still attached to the cap, protecting the gills.

Above

The skirtlike ring of the Deathcap (*Amanita phalloides*) is relatively fleeting.

Right

The stem of this Golden Cap (*Phaeolepiota aurea*) is sheathed in an armilla that terminates in a magnificent, ample skirtlike ring. This species grows mainly in grassy areas in the mountains.

Above

Another beautiful example of a pendant ring, in the Fly
Agaric (*Amanita muscaria*). In this specimen, the white
flakes usually left on the cap have disappeared, which
might cause it to be confused with Caesar's Mushroom.

Right

This Fly Agaric (*Amanita muscaria*) is a very
characteristic specimen, with its white flakes
arranged in a concentric pattern.

The Blusher (*Amanita rubescens*) comes in various forms. In the specimen to the right, the striations on the ring are clearly visible; they are the imprints left by the gills.

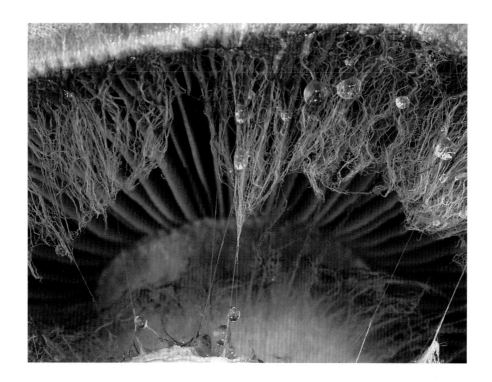

Above

Close-up of a cortina, with its filaments stretched between the cap and the stem. The rust-colored spores are clearly visible, especially around the stem.

Right

This Red Banded Webcap (*Cortinarius armillatus*) can be easily recognized by its bright, orange red, garlandlike annular traces. Its cap is ochraceous and covered with brownish red scales. This species often grows beneath birches.

The Slimy Spike (*Gomphidius glutinosus*) gets its name from its slimy veil, which is violet brown and acquires black spots as it ages. This species commonly grows beneath mountain spruce.

Spiny and Scaly Capped Mushrooms

In most capped mushrooms, the cap's cuticle (skin surface) is either smooth or feltlike. But mushroom caps vary tremendously in their texture, and each has a specific mycological designation – sometimes a technical-sounding term such as tomentose or hirsute, but other times a more down-to-earth description, such as downy, scaly or tousled.

One of the most remarkable examples of ornamented cuticles are the scaly type best exemplified by the larger species of *Lepiota*. In these species, the tissues beneath the cuticle develop more quickly than those at its surface, splitting them open into turned-up scales. But scales on mushroom caps come in other forms too, such as the pointy scales on many species of *Pholiota*. Such scales are an integral part of the cap itself and have nothing to do with the patches or warts sometimes left on mushroom caps as remnants of the universal veil.

Another very surprising-looking kind of mushroom cap occurs in certain species of puffball whose cuticles have long, sometimes curved spines, such as those of the Spiny Puffball, with its especially hirsute look.

The conical spines of this Common Puffball (*Lycoperdon perlatum*) are readily distinguished. They eventually slough off, leaving small circular marks called areolae. As in all gasteroid fungi, the inner flesh, known as the gleba, is initially firm but then breaks down into a powder: the mushroom's spores.

Preceding two-page spread, left

The caps and stems of these Shaggy Scalycaps (*Pholiota squarrosa*) are covered with brown scales against a lighter background. It is easy to see how the veil has been torn away to expose the gills.

Preceding two-page spread, right

The magnificent Flaming Scalycap (*Pholiota flammans*) often grows on dead conifers. The scales covering its cap and stem are initially almost yellow, but gradually darken to a rusty orange.

Above

With its numerous upturned scales, the Shaggy Parasol (*Chlorophyllum rhacodes*) certainly lives up to its name. It grows at the base of conifers. The easiest way to distinguish it with certainty from the Parasol Mushroom is to scratch its flesh, which then turns saffron red, and eventually brown.

Right

The Toothed Powdercap (*Flammulater muricatus*) is covered with fine, upright scales that are an attractive reddish brown color.

Left

The Common Puffball
(*Lycoperdon perlatum*) often
grows on the forest floor.

**Following two-page
spread, left**

The spines of the Umber-
brown Puffball (*Lycoperdon
umbrinum*) are much
shorter than those of
the Spiny Puffball.

**Following two-page
spread, right**

The spines of this Spring
Puffball (*Lycoperdon
echinatum*) are especially
long and curved, giving
it a curiously tousled
appearance. At maturity,
these spines slough off,
leaving hexagonal areolae.

Elegantly Capped Mushrooms

In mushrooms that have a distinct cap and stem, the shape of the cap does much to determine the mushroom's overall silhouette, which can be a great help in recognizing its species, or at least the group of species to which it belongs. But the cap's shape often changes as the mushroom grows. For example, in some clitocyboid mushrooms, the cap is initially convex, then flattens, then becomes more and more concave at the center, until it takes on a funnel-like shape such as the one that gives the Common Funnel its name.

The endless variety of mushroom cap shapes is reflected in the highly specific terminology that mycologists always use to describe the shape of the cap of each species at every stage of its development as accurately as they can. These shapes range from highly convex (virtually cylindrical, for example, in the young Shaggy Ink Cap) to highly concave (such as the cornucopia shape of the Horn of Plenty). In between, some mushrooms have pretty little caps shaped like bells, whereas others, such as amanitas, have caps with the classic parasol shape. There are even some mushrooms whose caps curl up at the edges as they age, until they look like a twirling skirt.

Like many other species of *Lactarius,* the Fenugreek Milk Cap (*Lactarius helvus*) has a cap shaped like a crater. This species grows readily beneath conifers and birches and is often found in sphagnum moss.

Left

The oblong cap of the Firerug Inkcap (*Coprinellus domesticus*) is covered in a powdery veil with small pyramidal scales. This veil is temporary and disappears fairly quickly. This species grows in clusters on decaying hardwood logs, and sometimes even on indoor carpets, hence its name.

Right

With its bell-shaped cap and long stem, the Milking Bonnet (*Mycena galopus*) makes a very elegant appearance. When broken, the stem exudes a milky white fluid.

Left

The Mountain Brownie, or Magic Mushroom (*Psilocybe bohemica*) belongs to a group of highly toxic mushrooms. It turns completely blue when handled.

Right

The Deer Shield (*Pluteus flavofuligineus*) has a very unusual color. The indentations in its cap are also unusual, and probably due to obstacles encountered while it was growing.

Following double-page spread, left

The Green Brittlegill (*Russula aeruginea*) has the most classic shape for a mushroom cap: a parasol; it spreads out with age. This mushroom grows beneath birch and spruce.

Following double-page spread, right

This Blackedged Shield (*Pluteus atromarginatus*) has a somewhat dented cap. This photo might suggest that it grows in mosses, but it actually grows on dead conifer branches (there is surely one beneath the mosses pictured here).

Above

The Common Funnel Cap (*Clitocybe gibba*) can be easily recognized by its funnel-shaped cap (often with a nipple in the center), as well as its smooth, silky surface, its gills running down the stem and its distinctive odor.

Right

The Horn of Plenty (*Craterellus cornucopioides*), or Black Trumpet, has a funnel-shaped cap that is hollow all the way down to the base of the stem and irregularly crisped and wavy at the margin.

The wavy-edged caps of
the Russet Toughshank
(*Gymnopus dryophilus*)
above and the *Cortinarius*
to the right are reminiscent
of Marilyn Monroe's skirt
in the famous scene with
the subway grate.

Under the Cap

The vast majority of mushrooms with caps and stems belong to the phylum Basidiomycota, which gets its name from the basidia: the specialized, club-shaped cells that produce the spores in these species. The basidia constitute the hymenium (fertile surface) of the mushroom. In Basidiomycota, the hymenium is situated beneath the cap and comes in four main types: gilled, tubed, spined and false-gilled.

Gilled mushrooms are the most numerous and include genera such as *Amanita*, *Cortinarius* and *Russula*. Often, between the gills, there are lamellae, and between them, lamellulae, with all of these elements radiating outward from the stem. This overall structure is an excellent way of increasing the mushroom's fertile surface area; a Portobello mushroom for example, can thus produce several million spores.

Tubed mushrooms are far less numerous. They include the polypore family and the large family of boletes (except for the Golden-gilled Bolete, which, as its name implies, has a form of gills). The tubes of these mushrooms look like organ pipes, and the spores are inside them. At maturity, the spores escape from pores — openings on the underside of the cap that make it look something like a sponge or, when they grow larger, like a honeycomb.

Slightly less numerous than tubed mushrooms, but more spectacular, the mushrooms with spiny hymenia comprise several families. The best known representative of this group is the Wood Hedgehog.

The least abundant group are the false-gilled mushrooms. In some false-gilled species, such as the chanterelle, the false gills are salient enough to resemble true gills. But in *Craterellus* species, such as the Horn of Plenty, they are much less pronounced, and the hymenia are described as "wrinkled" or "ridged."

Left

The Velvety Milk Cap (*Lactarius lignyotus*) has white, widely spaced gills that contrast with its dark cap and stem. This species is fairly rare and grows only beneath spruce in the mountains.

Following two-page spread

The broad, white, adnate gills of these Velvet Shanks (*Flammulina velutipes*) make a lovely contrast with their brown, velvety stems. This mushroom grows in clusters on hardwoods.

Above

In *Hygrophorus* species, especially the Blistered Woodwax (*Hygrophorus pustulatus*), the gills are thick and quite widely spaced.

Right

The aptly named Grooved Bonnet (*Mycena polygramma*) is easily recognized by the longitudinal grooves on its stem. Its gills range in color from white to grayish and acquire rust brown stains as they age.

Above

The Tawny Funnel Cap (*Lepista flaccida*) has pale
tawny gills that are crowded and deeply decurrent.

Right

The Lung Oyster (*Pleurotus pulmonarius*) has a short,
lateral stem. It grows in clusters on hardwood trunks.

Following two-page spread

Beneath its velvety cap, the
gills of the Velvet Rollrim
(*Tapinella atrotomentosa*)
turn from cream-colored
to ochraceous with age.
They are relatively thick
and can be easily broken off
the cap with a fingernail.

Above

The gills of the Fragrant Funnel (*Clitocybe fragrans*) are not separated at the stem.

Right

The red gills of the Bloodred Webcap (*Cortinarius sanguineus*) turn cinnamon brown when the spores mature. This species is toxic.

The Dusky Bolete
(*Porphyrellus porphyrosporus*)
is a rare species. Its
hymenium is covered with
small openings — the
pores at the end of its
tubes. The velvety cap is
a muddy brownish gray
with a tinge of purple.

**Following two-page
spread, left**

Unlike the tubes of boletes,
the tubes of polypores cannot
be separated from the cap.
In this Pie Goat mushroom
(*Scutiger pescaprae*), they
are short and decurrent, and
the pores are hexagonal.

**Following two-page
spread, right**

The whitish to cream-colored
pores of the Spring Polypore
(*Polyporus arcularius*)
form large polygons. This
mushroom is parasitic. Its
cap is covered with brown
scales and sometimes
grows to a diameter of
23⅝ inches (60 cm).

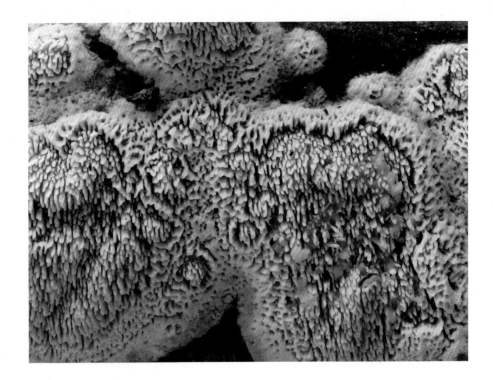

Above

This Split Porecrust (*Schizopora paradoxa*) is characteristic
of the species, with its highly irregular pores that
sometimes turn into spines and form a sort of labyrinth.

Left

The Ocher Bracket (*Trametes ochracea*) has
whitish, round, regular pores, and a thickness
of about ⅜ of an inch (10 mm).

Preceding two-page spread

The Lumpy Bracket
(*Trametes gibbosa*) is a very
common mushroom. Its
spores, often rectangular,
are clearly visible on
these young specimens.

Right

Excellent to eat, the
Wood Hedgehog (*Hydnum
repandum*) is unquestionably
the best known mushroom
with a spiny hymenium.

Above

The Terracotta Hedgehog (*Hydnum rufescens*) is much more orange than the Wood Hedgehog and has a central stem. It is also smaller and less fleshy, but just as good to eat.

Left

The Black Tooth (*Phellodon niger*) resembles the Wood Hedgehog somewhat. Its spines are bluish and run down the stem.

The Spruce Tooth (*Bankera violascens*) could just as easily have been placed in the chapter on colorful mushrooms. The lilac hue of all its parts is remarkable, especially when it is young.

Above

The Earpick Fungus (*Auriscalpium vulgare*) has a frail, lateral stem and relatively long, conical spines.

Right

The white to cream-colored spines of the Orange Tooth (*Hydnellum floriforme*) contrast boldly with its orange stem.

The Jelly Tooth
(*Pseudohydnum gelatinosum*)
is completely soft (even
its spines), which makes
it impossible to confuse
with any other *Hydnum*. Its
cap is brownish gray, and
its spines are whitish.

Above

The Devil's Tooth (*Hydnellum peckii*) exudes droplets ranging in color from vermilion to brownish red, which leave dark orange stains on its velvety surface. Its cap, pure white in younger specimens, soon turns a creamy pink.

Right

The cap and spines of this young Blue Tooth (*Hydnellum caeruleum*) are sky blue, but the blue quickly fades, then turns white. This species is found only at high elevations.

Above

The delicious Chanterelle (*Cantharellus cibarius*) does not have true gills; the folds visible here contain the cells that produce its spores.

Left

The Trumpet Chanterelle (*Craterellus tubaeformis*) is good to eat. It has a grayish hymenium composed of false gills that fork frequently. The cap is lobed, funnel-shaped and brownish gray, whereas the stem is yellow.

Above

The hymenium of the Black Trumpet (*Craterellus cornucopioides*) is fairly rudimentary. As seen here, it has no gills, tubes, spines or even false gills. The outer surface simply has shallow wrinkles; it whitens as the spores mature.

Right

The Pig's Ear (*Gomphus clavatus*) quickly turns bright violet. Its hymenium is irregular, wrinkled and veined. It is good to eat, but rare, and hence deserves protection.

Cup Mushrooms

Just as Basidiomycota take their name from the basidia – the specialized cells that produce their spores — Ascomycota, the other major phylum of "higher fungi," take their name from the asci — the elongated cells that produce theirs. There are far more species of Ascomycota than Basidiomycota. Many Ascomycota are cup-shaped, with the hymenium forming the inner surface of the cup. Cup mushrooms belong to the family Pezizaceae, with many species in the type genus, *Peziza*. They generally grow on the ground or on rotting wood, and they vary in size. Their colors also vary and are especially vivid in several species, such as the Scarlet Elf Cup, which gets its name from the very bright red inner surface of its cup.

In Pezizaceae species, the cup may rest directly on the substrate or may be supported by a stem that varies in length. The cup may sprawl open or be closed inward. Its margin may be smooth, or it may be jagged, as in some *Geopora* that have a pretty, crownlike shape. The cup may also be slightly or heavily deformed and in some species may even stand up straight like a rabbit's ear. The diversity of shapes in cup fungi is truly impressive.

Pseudoaleuria fibrillosa grows in sandy soils. The inner surface is orange, whereas the outer surface is covered with small hairs and turns a lighter color.

Above

Peziza grow first in the shape of a cup, then flatten out. This individual has a shiny, ocher hymenium and an exterior dotted with small, darker warts. This genus is often found around fire pits.

Left

The splendid Corona Cup (*Plectania melastoma*) grows in colonies on fallen deadwood.

The Golden Cup (*Caloscypha fulgens*) is a rare species and a true work of art. Its brilliant orange interior complements its greenish yellow exterior beautifully.

Right

The Glazed Cup (*Humaria hemisphaerica*) often grows half-buried in the ground. Its hymenium is blue gray, with brown hairs around the margin. The outer surface is ocher and also is covered with brown hairs.

Following two-page spread, left

The Anemone Cup (*Dumontinia tuberosa*), is about 1¼ inches (3 cm) in diameter and grows best in spring, in wet woodlands, together with the Wood Anemone (*Anemone nemorosa*).

Following two-page spread, right

The Ebony Cup (*Pseudoplectania nigrella*) has a very shiny black hymenium. It grows in spring, on moss cushions near conifer stumps and on soil covered with conifer needles.

Left

The fruiting body of this Black Bulgar (*Bulgaria inquinans*) is still globular but will soon spread open to expose a black hymenium. Touching the spores will leave serious stains on your fingers!

Right

The Devil's Urn (*Urnula craterium*) initially grows in a bell-like shape, then opens out into the form of a vase, with a ragged margin. Its stem varies in length and is sometimes hard to discern in the moss. It grows in winter and spring on buried wood.

Before assuming the crown shape seen to the left, the Sand Cup (*Geopora arenicola*) grows half-buried, as shown above.

107

Above

Before it opens up, the Rosy
Goblet (*Microstoma protracta*)
grows in the tight orange
cup shape seen here.

Right

Looking for all the world like
a bouquet of flowers, the
rare Rosy Goblet (*Microstoma
protracta*), is a magnificent
scarlet color. It often grows
in groups on humus, in
hardwood and mixed forests.

Sponge and Coral Mushrooms

With mushrooms, you can expect the unexpected. Some mushrooms look so much like sponges or corals that you feel as if you've suddenly plunged beneath the waves. Oddly enough, some mushrooms share another characteristic with sponges and corals: they grow in association with algae. In mushrooms, this kind of association produces lichens, but the mushrooms that form lichens have nothing to do with the ones that we are discussing here, which resemble sponges and corals in shape and appearance only.

Examples of spongelike mushrooms include a few species in the family Sparassidaceae, of which *Sparassis crispa* is the type species. Other examples include morels and false morels, although the latter look somewhat more like brains than like sponges.

Mushrooms that resemble corals come in a wider variety and occur in several families, particularly Clavariaceae. Like corals, these mushrooms generally have branching structures of varying complexity. These branches are covered by the hymenium along their entire length. There are all kinds of coral-like mushrooms. One of the most spectacular is the Coral Tooth, whose indisputable beauty inspired the career of the famous Swedish mycologist Elias Fries.

The Cauliflower Mushroom (*Sparassis crispa*) can reach 15¾ inches (40 cm) in diameter, and some specimens can weigh as much as 22 pounds (10 kg)! This mushroom is much sought after for the table.

Left

Most false morels look more like brains, but the cap of this one, the Brown False Morel (*Gyromitra fastigiata*) has a more veinlike appearance.

Right

The very small Spring Hazel Cup (*Encoelia furfuracea*) occurs in clusters of several hollow, spherical vesicles. In this picture, not all of them have opened yet.

Above

Morels are the mushrooms that look the most like sponges.
The chambers, like a cluster of contiguous cup fungi,
give the cap as a whole its spongelike appearance. This
specimen is a Common Morel (*Morchella esculenta*).

Right

The pits of the Gray Morel (*Morchella vulgaris*) are
black inside, whereas the ridges are a lighter color.

The Goldfinger Fungus
(*Ramaria pallidosaponaria*)
looks something like a
sponge and something like
a coral. It is usually pale
yellow, but sometimes
takes on ocher tones.

Left

The Stinking Earthfan (*Thelephora palmata*) consists of numerous upright branches and can be recognized by its rotten-cabbage smell.

Right

This very elegant Strict-Branch Coral (*Ramaria stricta*) looks as if it is growing on the sea bottom.

Following two-page spread

The Stag's Horn (*Xylaria hypoxylon*) is very common in stands of hardwood, especially beech. Its branches are smooth and black, with a dusting of white toward the top, and rosy tips, like tiny flames.

Above

The Crimped Gill (*Plicaturopsis crispa*) is initially resupinate (with the underside facing up) and has flat, thin folds that are white to light ocher and often forked. It resembles certain corals.

Right

As it ages, the Bearded Tooth (*Hericium flagellum*) acquires a pink tinge that makes it look more and more like a coral.

It would be hard for any mushroom to look more like white coral than this Coral Spine (*Hericium clathroides*).

Colorful Mushrooms

The most common colors for mushrooms are yellow, ocher, brown and white, in many different shades. But mushrooms also come in shades of red, blue (the least common), violet, green, gray, black and even black and white. There are also some bioluminescent mushrooms, which usually emit green light, but this is a rather rare phenomenon and involves only about 70 species. Most of them occur in tropical countries, but there are almost 20, including the largest living organism in the world, the "humungous fungus" (*Armillaria solidipes*) that can be found in North America.

The colors of mushrooms are often alluded to in their names, such as Honey Mushroom, Blood Bolete, Violet Chanterelle, Orange Peel Fungus, Amethyst Deceiver, Rosy Bonnet, Green Elfcup and Gilded Brittlegill. Some genera, such as *Russula, Hygrophorus* and *Cortinarius,* include numerous brightly colored species.

Mushrooms get their colors from pigments that are located mainly in the surface layers of their caps. A mushroom's color sometimes comes from a single pigment, but more often from a mixture. Colors are generally specific to a species, but can also vary among individuals, as well as with age, available moisture and other factors. Also, in some species, the flesh changes color rapidly when cut open. The Bluing Bolete, for example, changes from cream colored to an intense blue. Other mushrooms turn yellow, red, pink, black or some other color.

The Parrot Toadstool (*Hygrocybe psittacina*) is covered in slime. Its cap has a striated margin. Its overall color is a pretty parrot green, but it can also turn yellow or red. It grows mainly in grasslands but is also found in the forest.

Above

Except for its snow white color, the European Destroying Angel (*Amanita virosa*) is almost identical to the Death Cap (*Amanita phalloides*). Its stem is fuzzy, and its cap is bell-shaped and slightly tilted to one side. This specimen is not yet mature.

Right

The Bitter Bracket (*Oligoporus stipticus*) has a pure white, velvety cuticle. Initially an inverted cone, the cap spreads out into a fan shape, its underside covered with fine pores.

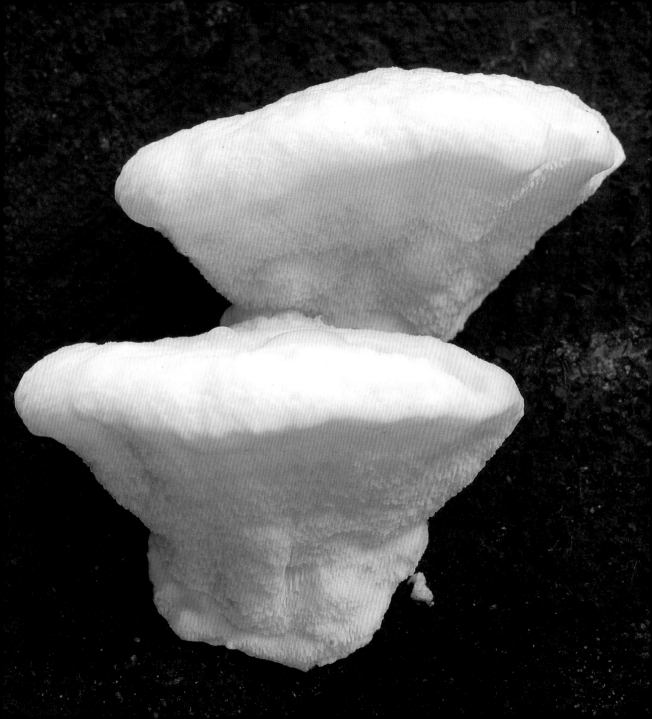

Above

The Yellow Brain Fungus or Witch's Butter (*Tremella mesenterica*) is a pretty, bright yellow. This oddly gelatinous mushroom grows in hardwood forests.

Left

Waxcaps come in a beautiful palette of colors and many different shades, like the orange yellow of this Persistent Waxcap (*Hygrocybe acutoconica*).

Above

The Small Staghorn Fungus (*Calocera cornea*) is a pretty little golden yellow mushroom that grows on decaying hardwood. Its fruiting bodies can be simple or forked. They become very slippery and shiny in wet weather.

Right

These young Spectacular Rustgills (*Gymnopilus spectabilis*) are not yet fully developed but already display their characteristic rusty ocher color.

Above

The magnificent Golden Waxgill (*Hygrophorus aureus*) has a vermilion cap.

Right

The fiery-colored Bitter Waxcap (*Hygrocybe mucronella*) gets its Latin species name from its mucrons – the small, pointed teeth around the rim of its cap.

Following two-page spread, left

The beautiful Orange Peel Fungus (*Aleuria aurantia*) grows in numerous clusters on the ground. Some cooks sprinkle it with cherry liqueur and serve it as an appetizer.

Following two-page spread, right

The Scarlet Elf Cup (*Sarcoscypha jurana*), with its searing red color, grows in winter and spring. What a nice surprise to find one beneath the branches of a blackthorn or hawthorn!

Above

The bright red cap of The Sickener (*Russula emetica*) stands out against the green sphagnum mosses in which it grows. It is found in wet habitats, beneath mountain conifers.

Right

The big, beautiful Red-Tinted Russula (*Russula paludosa*) grows in peat bogs. Its cap is deep red, slick and shiny.

Above

This Plums and Custard (*Tricholomopsis rutilans*) is
a characteristic purple red. The surfaces of the cap
and stem gradually yellow and develop scales.

Right

The Verdigris Roundhead (*Stropharia
aeruginosa*) is a lovely blue green.

Above

The Violet Webcap (*Cortinarius violaceus*) is easy to recognize. It is uniformly deep violet and has a downy cap. The stem base is swollen and sometimes has veil remnants that catch the spores fallen from the gills.

Left

The Wood Blewit (*Lepista nuda*) is a very late mushroom and grows even after the first frosts. Completely lilac blue at first, it grows paler with age and assumes russet tones. It is very good to eat.

Right

As the stem of the Girdled Webcap (*Cortinarius trivialis*) grows longer, it causes a series of ruptures in its encasing veil. The result is a series of belts composed of very slimy mucus.

Left

As its Latin name suggests, the Porcelain Fungus or Poached Egg Fungus (*Oudemansiella mucida*) has a very viscid surface. It grows in clumps on beeches and becomes really sticky in the rain.

Above

Earthtongue mushrooms
get their name from their
habitat and their tonguelike
shape. This specimen
is a Plain Earthtongue
(*Geoglossum umbratile*).

Right

The hymenium of the
Ebony Cup (*Pseudoplectania
nigrella*) is solid black.

Mushrooms That Grow on Wood

Mushrooms are found in all kinds of habitats, including grasslands, but are generally associated with the woods. Fungi and wood do have a long history together. Part of it is that the roots of most trees live in symbiosis with the mycelium (underground portion) of one or more species of fungus. That is why experienced hunters know which kinds of mushrooms they can expect to find at the foot of which kinds of trees. But many species of mushrooms grow directly on wood. Saprophytic mushrooms live on dead wood and other decomposing organic matter. Parasitic mushrooms feed on living wood, and some of them can become saprophytes once their host has died.

The variety of mushrooms that grow on wood is impressive, and all of these species help to break down dead wood, a process essential for the health of forest ecosystems. Among the best known are the polypores, which grow on tree trunks and include the famous Tinder Fungus, used to start fires since prehistoric times. Another is the Judas's Ear, which is nothing more than a variety of black mushroom.

Mushrooms that grow on wood also include some tiny species that will colonize even the smallest amount of tree debris. For example, the miniscule Holly Parachute grows on dead leaves, whereas certain *Collybia*, such as the Sprucecone Cap, grow on spruce and pine cones lying on the ground. This miniature world has a beauty all its own.

The Chicken of the Woods (*Laetiporus sulphureus*) is one of the worst parasites of many trees (especially hardwoods). It is unusual in that it is brittle like plaster.

Above

The Stump Fairy Helmet (*Mycena stipata*) can be recognized by its ammonia smell and its striated cap. It grows in clusters on wood, in which its stem is sometimes buried.

Right

These small mushrooms with their bell-shaped caps are Winter Bonnets (*Mycena tintinnabulum*) and grow in the season from which they take their name.

Above

The Summer Bolete (*Bolbitius reticulatus* var. *pluteoides*) grows on small pieces of wood.

Right

The Yellow Fieldcap (*Bolbitius titubans* var. *olivaceus*) has prominent veins.

As these two pictures show, the Olive Oysterling (*Sarcomyxa serotina*) comes in a variety of colors. Its downy cap ranges from green to ocher yellow to red, depending on the climate.

Preceding two-page spread

The Cobalt Crust
(*Pulcherricium caeruleum*)
may be one of the most
striking of the species that
mycologists refer to as
crusts. It looks like cobalt
blue velvet, with lighter
tones around its margins. It
grows on fallen hardwoods.

Left

Ossicaulis lignatilis somewhat
resemble Oyster Mushrooms
in shape, are generally
white and tend to grow
in northern habitats.

Right

These young Oyster
Mushrooms (*Pleurotus
ostreatus*) have decurrent
gills extended by a
net on the stem.

Above

In very dry conditions, the split gills of *Schizophyllum commune* close to protect the hymenium.

Right

The cap of the Common Mazegill (*Datronia mollis*) is often attached to the wood by a small surface. The pores are alveolate and uneven. As they age, they become elongated and dentate, forming a maze.

Above

The Artist's Bracket
(*Ganoderma lipsiense*)
sometimes grows to 23½
inches (60 cm). Its brown
upper surface is often
covered with spores. Its
underside is white and
covered with very fine pores.

Left

The Red-Belt Conk
(*Fomitopsis pinicola*)
is shaped like a thick
horseshoe, with concentric
zones. Every year, it produces
a layer of tubes that build up
in strata. It attacks weakened
trees and produces a red rot.

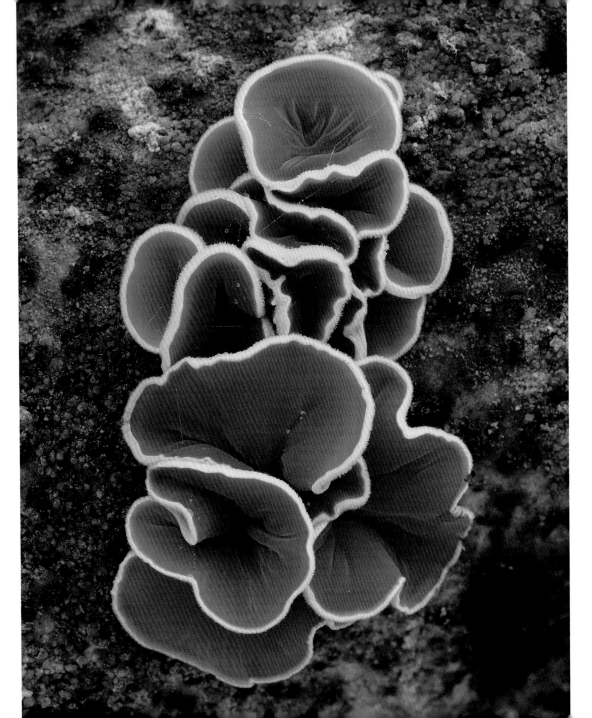

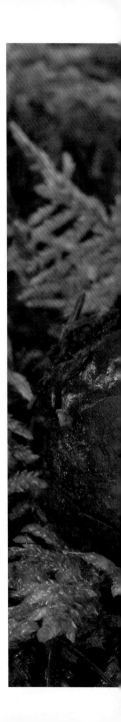

Above

Brown Cup (*Rutstroemia bulgarioides*) is a small mushroom that grows on cones of the spruce (*Picea abies*).

Right

As its name implies, the Conifercone Cap (*Baeospora myosura*) grows on fallen cones (mainly pine). It has an ochraceous stem covered with a light bloom. It can be distinguished from the other species resembling it by its crowded gills.

Preceding two-page spread, left

The fruiting body of *Schizophyllum amplum* is soft and gelatinous. The hymenium is brownish ocher, with pronounced veins. This species grows mostly on poplar trunks.

Preceding two-page spread, right

This Dryad's Saddle (*Polyporus squamosus*) seems to grow in a spiral. Its pores are clearly visible all the way to the stem. It works its way into wounds, often at forks between branches.

Bizarre Mushrooms

Mushrooms come in an extremely wide variety of forms, often quite different from the stem and parasol cap that we think of as the classic mushroom silhouette. In addition to the veiled, cup, sponge and coral mushrooms seen in the preceding chapters, mushrooms come in almost any shape you can imagine—balls, buttons, nests, fans, clubs, boots, crusts, tongues, phalluses, ears, trumpets, lanterns, octopi and stars. That's not even counting the exotic species — the variety is virtually endless.

What we commonly call a mushroom is actually only the reproductive part of the fungus and is scientifically known as the sporophore. (The vegetative portion of the fungus, the mycelium, is usually underground.) The sporophore's sole purpose is to produce and scatter its spores. The sporophore is to the fungus as the flower is to the plant.

In Ascomycota, which include morels, elfin saddles, microglossums and many other strangely shaped species, the asci simply eject the spores. In many Basidiomycota, the stem, by holding the cap up off the ground, makes it easier for the wind to carry the spores away. But in gasteroid ("stomach") fungi, the outer surfaces of the mushroom are sterile; the spores are produced on the inside, and their dissemination may require outside intervention. That is why all of the spectacularly phallic mushrooms, such as the Common Stinkhorn and the Octopus Stinkhorn, give off a stench that very effectively attracts the flies that will carry their spores away. In some other gasteroid fungi, such as puffballs and earthstars, the spores are released through openings called ostioles, but the process is often helped along by the pressure exerted by passing animals or people.

The Octopus Stinkhorn (*Clathrus archeri*) is a truly strange-looking mushroom, somewhat resembling the mollusk from which it takes its name. It gives off an odor of rotting flesh, thus attracting insects to spread its spores.

Above

The fertile portion of the Olive Earthtongue (*Microglossum viride*) is in the upper part of the plant. The stem is pale olive green to dark green and often has longitudinal furrows.

Right

The Snaketongue Truffleclub (*Cordyceps ophioglossoides*) is a parasite of the Deer Truffle (*Elaphomyces granulatus*) and is often found in mosses at the foot of conifers.

Above

Jelly Babies (*Leotia lubrica*) are a toxic species. Their
lobed caps may cause them to be mistaken for young
Trumpet Chanterelles (*Craterellus tubaeformis*).

Right

The Elastic Saddle (*Helvella elastica*) has a saddle-shaped
cap and, often, a hollowed-out stem, as seen here. It
is sometimes found at the sides of roads and paths.

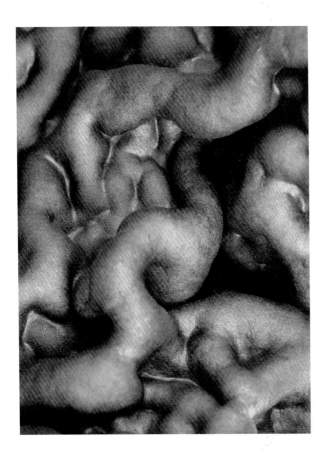

The False Morel (*Gyromitra esculenta*) is very toxic when raw or inadequately cooked. It is something like a morel with a brain-shaped cap.

Left

The Giant Club or Pestle Fungus (*Clavariadelphus pistillaris*) looks like a club with a rounded end. Initially yellow, it turns ocher first, and then red.

Right

The Judas's Ear or Jelly Ear (*Auricularia auricula-judae*) grows in Europe on the wood of deciduous trees and shrubs, especially elderberry.

Preceding two-page spread

The Black Witches' Butter or Black Jelly (*Exidia glandulosa*) likes to come out in wet weather. Once established, usually on deadwood, it gradually spreads out in an irregular blob. Its fertile surface, the hymenium, is black (either shiny or matte, depending on the climate).

Left

The Dog Stinkhorn (*Mutinus caninus*), like the Common Stinkhorn, is hard to miss in the forest. For one thing, its odor is perceptible from a distance. For another, its shape is eye-catching, to say the least!!

Right

The Dune Stinkhorn (*Phallus hadriani*) is a dead ringer for the Common Stinkhorn (*Phallus impudicus*), much more common, and with a whitish volva.

Above

As its genus name suggests, the Common Earthball
(*Scleroderma citrinum*) has a hard, dry "skin." It
is very elastic at first, then becomes powdery.
It is covered with small brown scales.

Right

The ball-shaped False Truffle (*Rhizopogon
roseolus*) grows mainly on conifers. It is
ochraceous but turns red when bruised.

Following two-page spread, right

The Fringed Earthstar or Sessile Earthstar (*Geastrum fimbriatum*) has six to nine thick, downward-curving rays. The spore case, at the center, has an apical pore that opens to release the spores.

Following two-page spread, left

Earthstars are like puffballs with multiple peridia. The Rayed Earthstar (*Geastrum quadrifidum*) looks like a flower with four petals.

Above and right

The Dyeball or Dead Man's Foot (*Pisolithus arrhizus*) is a very odd mushroom. It has a sporophore measuring 1¼ inches (3 to 10 cm) but a very short stem. Its gleba is divided into chambers that, in cross-section, look like an irregular gravel pavement.

The Field Earthstar
(*Geastrum pouzarii*) has a
fimbriate ostiole (one with
stripes on its margin). The
specimen above is unusual
in having two ostioles.

Above

Earthstars are a sort of double puffball. The outer layer of the spore case of this Berkeley's Earthstar (*Geastrum berkeleyi*) has split open like a star or flower.

Right

The Weather Earthstar (*Geastrum corollinum*) has numerous brown rays.

Adnate: lamellae or tubes broadly attached to the stipe.

Adnexed: lamellae partially attached to the stipe.

Amyloid: stained blue by iodine.

Annulus: the ring shaped veil remnant on a mushroom stalk.

Apiculus: a projection at the base of the basidiospores where the spore is attached to the sterigmata, also referred to as the hilar appendage.

Appressed: pressed closely or fitting closely to something.

Basidia: it is the structure on which the sexual spores are borne.

Bulbous: bulblike or having a swelling at the base of the stipe.

Campalanate/campanulate: bell shaped.

Clamp connection: a looplike structure located at the septa of the hyphae.

Clavate: club shaped or having one end thickened.

Concolorous: same color throughout.

Conifer: a tree with needles or scales such as pine; also called an evergreen.

Convoluted: coiled up to form a twisted shape.

Cortina: a cobweblike partial veil of some mushrooms.

Costate: ribbed.

Crenate: scalloped.

Cuticle: outer skin or layer of the mushroom stipe or pileus.

Decurrent: extending down the stipe of a mushroom.

Decurve (incurve): bent downwards.

Eccentric: a stipe not attached in the center of the cap.

Ellipsoidal: bilaterally symmetrical with curved sides and rounded ends.

Evanescent: appearing briefly then vanishing.

Farinaceous: covered with mealy flourlike particles; also smelling or tasting like fresh flour.

Fibril: minute hair.

Fibrillose: covered with silky fibers.

Fissured: a long narrow opening, a crack or a cleft.

Floccose: covered with tufts of soft cottony hair.

Flocculose: fine cottony.

Furcate: forked.

Fusiform: tapering at one or both ends; spindle shaped.

Glabrous: lacking hairs, warts or scales.

Globose: round.

Glutinous: (the layer on cap or stalk) slimy; in wet weather sometimes oozing or hanging from the margin of the cap

Gregarious: a number of fruiting bodies growing in groups.

Hardwood: tree with broad leaves eg., elm, maple or birch.

Hemispherical: having the form of half a sphere.

Hyaline: glassy or transparent.

Hygrophanous: transparent when wet and opaque when dry.

Hymenium: spore bearing surface such as the gills of a mushroom, pores of boletes, head of morels.

Hyphae: one or more fungal cells, collectively called as a mycelium.

Intervenose: veined in the interspaces.

Lamellae: one of the radiating vertical plates on the underside of the cap of an agaric mushroom; also called gills.

Latex: a variously colored juice; present in *Lactarius* tissue.

Marginate: having a border or edge with a distinct color or pattern.

Mealy: smelling of fresh grain or having a granular appearance.

Membranous: skinlike tissue making up the partial veil of some mushrooms.

Mycelium: collective name for the filaments of the vegetative fungus plant.

Obliquely: slanting to a side, diverging from a given straight line.

Ovoid: egg shaped.

Partial veil: a covering that extends from the unopened margin of the mushroom cap to the stalk.

Pileus: the horizontal portion of a mushroom, bearing gills or tubes on the underside.

Plane: having a flat surface.

Pruinose: covered with a fine powder.

Reticulate: shallow, netlike ridges; a series of connected ridges.

Reticulum: is a netlike arrangement over the surface of the stipe, pileus or spore.

Rhizomorph: a dense mass of hyphae forming a rootlike structure.

Septum: cross wall in a fungus cell.

Sinuate: (of gills) notched at the stalk.

Squamules: small scales.

Sterigmata: a small stalk that bears a spores.

Stipe: the stalk or stem supporting the pileus of the mushroom.

Striate: striped, grooved or ridged.

Sulcate: having narrow deep furrows or grooves.

Superior: situated near the top part.

Tapering: a gradual decrease in thickness or width of an elongated object.

Tenacious: adhesive or sticky.

Terete: cylindrical or slightly tapering.

Tomentose: densely hairy, wooly.

Umbo: a blunt or rounded central swelling (on top of a pileus).

Umbonate: with an umbo.

Universal veil: a tissue surrounding the developing mushroom button.

Vinaceous: color of red wine.

Viscid: covered by a sticky substance.

Volva: cuplike structure around the base of the stalk of certain mushrooms.

Warts: unattached pieces of the universal veil that remain on the cap of some mushrooms; a type of ornamentation on spore walls.

Zonate: having concentric bands or zones of color.

Important Poisoning Disclaimer

The content in this book is for information and interest only. It is not an identification guide to mushrooms and fungi and it should not be interpreted as such. Many mushrooms are poisonous and some are deadly poisonous. We have made every effort to ensure accuracy but the responsibility for eating any mushroom or fungus rests solely with the individual, including any outcome due to allergy or intolerance for any mushroom or fungus, whatever the species. If you collect any mushrooms to eat make sure that your identification checks out in every detail. Never eat any wild mushroom until an expert mycologist has checked your identification. Even when you know a mushroom well, weather conditions or animal damage can cause differences in appearance that could lead to misidentification.

Note: Reference to "Europe" includes the European continent and the United Kingdom of Great Britain and Northern Ireland.

Page:	102
Common Name:	**Anemone Cup**
Scientific Name:	*Dumontinia tuberosa* syn *Sclerotinia tuberosa*
Size:	Less than 3 cm
Distribution:	North America, Europe. Associated with Wood Anemone (*Anemone nemorosa*)
Edibility:	Inedible

Page:	162–163
Common Name:	**Artist's Bracket**
Scientific Name:	*Ganoderma lipsiense*
Size:	Up to 60 cm
Distribution:	North America, Europe
Edibility:	Inedible

Page:	123
Common Name:	**Bearded Tooth**
Scientific Name:	*Hericium flagellum*
Size:	15–30 cm
Distribution:	North America, Europe
Edibility:	Edible

Page:	190
Common Name:	**Berkeley's Earthstar**
Scientific Name:	*Geastrum berkeleyi*
Size:	Less than 5 cm
Distribution:	Europe
Edibility:	Inedible

Page:	128–129
Common Name:	**Bitter Bracket**
Scientific Name:	*Postia stiptica* syn *Oligoporus stipticus*
Size:	To 10 cm wide
Distribution:	North America, Europe, Asia
Edibility:	Edible

Page:	135
Common Name:	**Bitter Waxcap**
Scientific Name:	*Hygrocybe mucronella*
Size:	Cap 1–4 cm, stem 4–5 cm
Distribution:	North America, Europe
Edibility:	Inedible

Page:	104
Common Name:	**Black Bulgar**
Scientific Name:	*Bulgaria inquinans*
Size:	Less than 5 cm
Distribution:	North America, Europe
Edibility:	Inedible

Page:	80–81
Common Name:	**Black tooth**
Scientific Name:	*Phellodon niger*
Size:	Cap 3–8 cm, stem 1–5 cm
Distribution:	North America, Europe. Rare.
Edibility:	Edibility unknown

Page:	92
Common Name:	**Black Trumpet**
Scientific Name:	*Craterellus cornucopioides*
Size:	Funnel 4–8 cm
Distribution:	North America, Europe, Asia
Edibility:	Edible

Page:	178–179
Common Name:	**Black Witches' Butter, Black Jelly**
Scientific Name:	*Exidia glandulosa*
Size:	2–6 cm
Distribution:	North America, Europe
Edibility:	Inedible

Page:	53
Common Name:	**Blackedged Shield**
Scientific Name:	*Pluteus atromarginatus*
Size:	Cap 3–10 cm, stem 5–10 cm
Distribution:	North America
Edibility:	Edible

Page:	62
Common Name:	**Blistered Woodwax**
Scientific Name:	*Hygrophorus pustulatus*
Size:	Cap 2–10 cm, stem 4–8 cm
Distribution:	North America, Europe
Edibility:	Edible

Page:	20, 30–31
Common Name:	**The Blusher**
Scientific Name:	*Amanita rubescens*
Size:	Cap 5–20, stem 6–15 cm
Distribution:	North America, Europe
Edibility:	Poisonous/suspect

Page:	89
Common Name:	**Blue Tooth**
Scientific Name:	*Hydnellum caeruleum*
Size:	3–11 cm wide, 5–15 cm tall
Distribution:	North America, Europe. Very Rare.
Edibility:	Inedible

Page:	69
Common Name:	**Bloodred Webcap**
Scientific Name:	*Cortinarius sanguineus*
Size:	Cap 2–5 cm, stem 3–8 cm
Distribution:	North America, Europe
Edibility:	Poisonous/suspect

Page: 10
Common Name: **Swamp Beacon**
Scientific Name: *Mitrula paludosa*
Size: Fruitbody 1 cm tall, stem less than 5 cm
Distribution: North America, Europe, Asia
Edibility: Inedible

Page: 166
Common Name: **Brown Cup**
Scientific Name: *Rutstroemia bulgarioides*
Size: Up to 3 cm
Distribution: Europe
Edibility: Edibility unknown

Page: 112
Common Name: **Brown False Morel**
Scientific Name: *Gyromitra fastigiata* syn *G. brunnea*
Size: Cap 3–10 cm, stem 5–10 cm
Distribution: North America, Europe, Asia
Edibility: Poisonous/suspect, easily confused with both edible and poisonous false morels. Only the very experienced should forage and prepare morels.

Page: 25
Common Name: **Bulbous Honey Fungus**
Scientific Name: *Armillaria gallica*
Size: Cap 4–10 cm, stem 5–15 cm
Distribution: Mainland Europe, North America, North Africa, Asia
Edibility: Poisonous/suspect

Page: 14
Common Name: **Caesar's Mushroom**
Scientific Name: *Amanita caesarea*
Size: Cap 6–18 cm, stem 5–15 cm
Distribution: Europe
Edibility: Edible

Page: 148
Common Name: **Chicken of the Woods**
Scientific Name: *Laetiporus sulphureus*
Size: Fruitbody 5–60 cm wide, 4 cm thick
Distribution: North America, Europe
Edibility: Edible if thoroughly cooked

Page: 4–5
Common Name: **Clouded Funnel**
Scientific Name: *Clitocybe nebularis* syn *Lepista nebularis*
Size: Cap 4–25 cm, stem 15 cm
Distribution: North America, Europe
Edibility: Poisonous/suspect, easily mistaken for poisonous *Entoloma sinuatum*

Page: 91
Common Name: **Chanterelle**
Scientific Name: *Cantharellus cibarius*
Size: Funnel 10 cm wide, stem 2 cm
Distribution: North America, Europe, Asia, Africa
Edibility: Edible

Page: 156–157
Common Name: **Cobalt Crust**
Scientific Name: *Pulcherricium caeruleum* syn *Terana caerulea*
Size: –
Distribution: North America, Europe, Asia, New Zealand
Edibility: Inedible

Page: 182
Common Name: **Common Earthball**
Scientific Name: *Scleroderma citrinum*
Size: 2–10 cm
Distribution: North America, Europe
Edibility: Inedible

Page: 54
Common Name: **Common Funnel Cap**
Scientific Name: *Clitocybe gibba*
Size: Cap 4–8 cm, stem 3–7 cm
Distribution: North America, Europe
Edibility: Edible

Page: 36, 42–43
Common Name: **Common Puffball**
Scientific Name: *Lycoperdon perlatum*
Size: 3–6 cm wide, 4–9 cm tall
Distribution: Worldwide
Edibility: Edible

Page: 161
Common Name: **Common Mazegill**
Scientific Name: *Datronia mollis*
Size: Up to 10 cm long, 3 cm wide, 0.6 cm thick
Distribution: North America, Europe
Edibility: Inedible

Page: 114
Common Name: **Common Morel**
Scientific Name: *Morchella esculenta*
Size: Cap 3–8 cm wide, 5–12 cm tall, stem 3–12 cm
Distribution: Northern Hemisphere regions
Edibility: Suspect, easily mistaken for poisonous false morels, *Gyromitra esculenta* Edible if cooked or dried

Page: 167
Common Name: **Conifercone Cap**
Scientific Name: *Baeospora myosura*
Size: Cap 1–3 cm, stem 3–5 cm
Distribution: North America, Europe
Edibility: Inedible

Page: 124–125
Common Name: **Coral Spine**
Scientific Name: *Hericium clathroides*
Size: 10–40 cm
Distribution: Europe, Australia and New Zealand
Edibility: Edible

Page: 96–97
Common Name: **Corona Cup**
Scientific Name: *Plectania melastoma*
Size: Less than 3 cm
Distribution: Northern Temperate Regions, West Indies, Australia, New Zealand, Mexico
Edibility: Edibility unknown

Page: 122
Common Name: **Crimped Gill**
Scientific Name: *Plicaturopsis crispa*
Size: Less than 5 cm
Distribution: Europe
Edibility: Inedible

Page: 9
Common Name: **Dark Honey Fungus**
Scientific Name: *Armillaria ostoyae*
Size: Cap 5–15 cm,
stem 5–15 cm,
underground up to
10 square km
Distribution: Europe, Asia, North
America, Australia,
New Zealand
Edibility: Edible/suspect

Page: 51
Common Name: **Deer Shield**
Scientific Name: *Pluteus flavofuligineus*
Size: Cap 2–8 cm, stem 4–10 cm
Distribution: North America
Edibility: Edible

Page: 26
Common Name: **Deathcap, Death Cup**
Scientific Name: *Amanita phalloides*
Size: Cap 5–15 cm, stem 7–15 cm
Distribution: Europe, Northern Africa,
Australia, South America,
Asia, North America
Edibility: Deadly *Aminata* fungi account
for more than 90% of deaths
from mushroom poisoning,
including the similar, all-white
Aminata phalloides var. *alba*

Page: 88
Common Name: **Devil's Tooth**
Scientific Name: *Hydnellum peckii*
Size: 3–8 cm wide, 3–10 cm tall
Distribution: North America, Europe
Edibility: Edibility unknown

Page: 105
Common Name: **The Devil's Urn**
Scientific Name: *Urnula craterium*
Size: 3–15 cm deep
Distribution: North America, Europe
Edibility: Inedible

Page: 180
Common Name: **Dog Stinkhorn**
Scientific Name: *Mutinus caninus*
Size: 10–20 cm
Distribution: North America, Europe, Asia
Edibility: Inedible

Page: 165
Common Name: **Dryad's Saddle**
Scientific Name: *Polyporus squamosus*
Size: 8–30 cm wide, 10 cm thick
Distribution: North America, Europe, Asia,
Australia
Edibility: Edible

Page: 181
Common Name: **Dune Stinkhorn**
Scientific Name: *Phallus hadriani*
Size: 10–18 cm
Distribution: North America, Europe
Edibility: Inedible

Page: p 70–71
Common Name: **Dusky Bolete**
Scientific Name: *Porphyrellus porphyrosporus*
Size: Cap 6–15 cm, stem 5–12 cm
Distribution: Europe
Edibility: Inedible

Page: 184
Common Name: **Dyeball, Dead Man's Foot**
Scientific Name: *Pisolithus arrhizus*
Size: 5–25 cm
Distribution: North America, Europe,
Australia
Edibility: Inedible

Page: 84
Common Name: **Earpick Fungus**
Scientific Name: *Auriscalpium vulgare*
Size: Cap 1–3 cm, stem 1–6 cm
Distribution: Central and North America,
Europe, Temperate Asia
Edibility: Inedible

Page: 103, 146–147
Common Name: **Ebony Cup**
Scientific Name: *Pseudoplectania nigrella*
Size: Less than 5 cm
Distribution: North America, Europe
Edibility: Inedible

Page: 173
Common Name: **Elastic Saddle**
Scientific Name: *Helvella elastica*
Size: Cap 1–3 cm high, stem 4–7 cm
Distribution: North America, Europe
Edibility: Inedible

Page: 128
Common Name: **European Destroying Angel**
Scientific Name: *Amanita virosa*
Size: Cap 5–12 cm, stem 9–12 cm
Distribution: North America, Europe
Edibility: Deadly poisonous. *Amanita
virosa* is one of the most
deadly mushrooms, the other
being *A. phalloides*, the Death
Cap. Immature specimens
resemble many edible fungi,
including *Agaricus arvensis* and
A. campestris, and the puffballs
Lycoperdon spp., increasing
the risk of accidental poisoning.
Avoid all *Amanita* fungi

Page: 22–23
Common Name: **False Deathcap**
Scientific Name: *Amanita citrina*
Size: Cap 5–10 cm, stem 6–10 cm
Distribution: North America, Europe.
Edibility: Suspect, easily mistaken for
deadly *Amanita* fungi such as
Destroying Angel.

Page: 174, 174–175
Common Name: **False Morel**
Scientific Name: *Gyromitra esculenta*
Size: Cap 3–11 cm, stem 2–5 cm
Distribution: North America, Europe
Edibility: Deadly poisonous, easily
confused with other morels,
especially edible *Morchella
esculenta*

Page: 182–183
Common Name: **False Truffle**
Scientific Name: *Rhizopogon roseolus*
Size: 1–6 cm
Distribution: North America, Europe
Edibility: Edible

Page: 46
Common Name: **Fenugreek Milk Cap**
Scientific Name: *Lactarius helvus*
Size: Cap 5–12 cm, stem 5–12 cm
Distribution: North America, Europe
Edibility: Poisonous/suspect

Page: 188–189, 189
Common Name: **Field Earthstar**
Scientific Name: *Geastrum pouzarii*
Size: Less than 5 cm
Distribution: Europe
Edibility: Inedible

Page: 48
Common Name: **Firerug Inkcap**
Scientific Name: *Coprinellus domesticus*
Size: Cap 7 cm, stem 4–15 cm
Distribution: Europe, North America
Edibility: Inedible

Page: 39
Common Name: **Flaming Scalycap**
Scientific Name: *Pholiota flammans*
Size: Cap 2–8 cm, stem 4–8 cm
Distribution: Europe, Asia, North America
Edibility: Inedible

Page: 28
Common Name: **Fly Agaric**
Scientific Name: *Amanita muscaria*
Size: Cap 10–20 cm, stem 10–25 cm
Distribution: Northern Hemisphere
Edibility: Deadly poisonous

Page: 68
Common Name: **Fragrant Funnel**
Scientific Name: *Clitocybe fragrans*
Size: Cap 1.5–4 cm, stem 3–6 cm
Distribution: North America, Europe
Edibility: Poisonous/suspect, easily mistaken for similar *Clitocybe* fungi, including the edible fragrant Aniseed Toadstool *Clitocybe odora*.

Page: 187
Common Name: **Fringed Earthstar, Sessile Earthstar**
Scientific Name: *Geastrum fimbriatum*
Size: Less than 5 cm
Distribution: The Americas, Europe, Africa, Asia, Australasia
Edibility: Inedible

Page: 24
Common Name: **Funeral Bell**
Scientific Name: *Galerina marginata*
Size: Cap 1.5–4 cm, stem 2–7 cm
Distribution: Europe, North America, Asia
Edibility: Deadly poisonous, easily mistaken for edible *Kuehneromyces mutabilis*

Page: 176
Common Name: **Giant Club, Pestle Fungus**
Scientific Name: *Clavariadelphus pistillaris*
Size: 8–30 cm
Distribution: North America, Europe
Edibility: Inedible

Page: 145
Common Name: **Girdled Webcap**
Scientific Name: *Cortinarius trivialis*
Size: Cap 4–11 cm, stem 5–12 cm
Distribution: North America, Europe
Edibility: Poisonous, easily mistaken for other toxic *Cortinarius* fungi

Page: 100–101
Common Name: **Glazed Cup**
Scientific Name: *Humaria hemisphaerica*
Size: Less than 5 cm
Distribution: North America, Europe
Edibility: Inedible

Page: 116–117
Common Name: **Goldfinger Fungus**
Scientific Name: *Ramaria pallidosaponaria* syn *R. flava*
Size: 10–20 cm high, 7–15 cm wide
Distribution: North America, Europe
Edibility: Edible, easily mistaken for several mildly poisonous fungi, including *Ramaria formosa* and *R. pallida*

Page: 27
Common Name: **Golden Bootleg, Golden Cap**
Scientific Name: *Phaeolepiota aurea*
Size: Cap 8–20 cm, stem 10–20 cm
Distribution: North America, Europe. Rare.
Edibility: Poisonous

Page: 98–99
Common Name: **Golden Cup**
Scientific Name: *Caloscypha fulgens*
Size: Less than 5 cm
Distribution: North America, Europe, Japan
Edibility: Edibility unknown

Page: 134
Common Name: **Golden Waxgill**
Scientific Name: *Hygrophorus aureus*
Size: Cap 2.5–10 cm, stem, 2–5 cm
Distribution: Europe
Edibility: Inedible

Page: 114–115
Common Name: **Gray Morel**
Scientific Name: *Morchella vulgaris*
Size: 5–15 cm
Distribution: Northern Hemisphere
Edibility: Suspect
Edible if cooked or dried

Page: 22
Common Name: **Gray Veiled Amanita**
Scientific Name: *Amanita porphyria*
Size: Cap 5–10 cm, stem 5–15 cm
Distribution: North America, Europe
Edibility: Poisonous/suspect

Page: 52
Common Name: **Green Brittlegill**
Scientific Name: *Russula aeruginea*
Size: Cap 4–9 cm, stem 4–8 cm
Distribution: North America, Europe
Edibility: Edible

Page: 63
Common Name: **Grooved Bonnet**
Scientific Name: *Mycena polygramma*
Size: Cap 2–3.5 cm, stem 5–10 cm
Distribution: North America, Europe
Edibility: Poisonous

Page: 54–55
Common Name: **Horn of Plenty**
Scientific Name: *Craterellus cornucopioides*
Size: Funnel 2–8 cm
Distribution: North America, Europe, Asia
Edibility: Edible

Page: 172
Common Name: **Jelly Babies**
Scientific Name: *Leotia lubrica*
Size: Fruitbody 1–4 cm wide, stem 2–5 cm
Distribution: North America, Europe
Edibility: Inedible

Page: 86–87
Common Name: **Jelly Tooth**
Scientific Name: *Pseudohydnum gelatinosum*
Size: 2–10 cm wide, up to 12 cm tall
Distribution: North America, Europe
Edibility: Inedible

Page: 177
Common Name: **Judas's Ear, Jelly Ear**
Scientific Name: *Auricularia auricula-judae*
Size: 3–8 cm
Distribution: Temperate regions worldwide
Edibility: Edible

Page: 76–77
Common Name: **Lumpy Bracket**
Scientific Name: *Trametes gibbosa*
Size: 5–20 cm wide, 1–6 cm thick
Distribution: North America, Europe
Edibility: Inedible

Page: 49
Common Name: **Milking Bonnet**
Scientific Name: *Mycena galopus*
Size: Cap 1–2.5 cm, stem 5–8 cm
Distribution: North America, Europe
Edibility: Inedible

Page: 50
Common Name: **Mountain Brownie, Magic Mushroom**
Scientific Name: *Psilocybe bohemica* syn *Pserbica* var *bohemica*
Size: Cap 5 cm, stem 5–15 cm
Distribution: North America, Europe
Edibility: Poisonous

Page: 74
Common Name: **Ocher Bracket**
Scientific Name: *Trametes ochracea*
Size: Cap 1.5–5 cm
Distribution: Europe
Edibility: Inedible

Page: 136
Common Name: **Orange Peel Fungus**
Scientific Name: *Aleuria aurantia*
Size: 5–15 cm
Distribution: North America, Europe
Edibility: Inedible

Page: 84–85
Common Name: **Orange Tooth**
Scientific Name: *Hydnellum floriforme*
Size: Up to 15 cm wide, 2–5 cm tall
Distribution: North America, Europe
Edibility: Inedible

Page: 154, 155
Common Name: **Olive Oysterling**
Scientific Name: *Sarcomyxa serotina*
Size: Cap 3–10 cm, stem 2 cm
Distribution: North America, Europe
Edibility: Inedible/suspect

Page: 158
Common Name: None
Scientific Name: *Ossicaulis lignatilis*
Size: Cap 1.5–5, stem 0.5–2 cm
Distribution: North America, Europe
Edibility: Edibility unknown

Page: 168
Common Name: **Octopus Stinkhorn, Devil's Fingers**
Scientific Name: *Clathrus archeri* syn *Anthurus archeri*
Size: 20 cm wide, 10 cm tall, 4–8 arms
Distribution: North America, Europe
Edibility: Inedible

Page: 170
Common Name: **Olive Earthtongue**
Scientific Name: *Microglossum viride*
Size: 1–2 cm long, 1 cm wide
Distribution: North America, Europe
Edibility: Inedible/suspect

Page: 159
Common Name: **Oyster Mushroom**
Scientific Name: *Pleurotus ostreatus*
Size: Cap 6–14 cm, stem 2–3 cm
Distribution: Temperate and subtropical forests worldwide
Edibility: Edible

Page: 65
Common Name: **Pale Oyster, Lung Oyster**
Scientific Name: *Pleurotus pulmonarius*
Size: Cap 2–10 cm, lateral stem
Distribution: North America, Europe
Edibility: Edible

Page: 126
Common Name: **Parrot Toadstool**
Scientific Name: *Hygrocybe psittacina*
Size: Cap 2–4 cm, stem 4–8 cm
Distribution: North America, Europe
Edibility: Inedible

Page: 19
Common Name: **Pearly Powdercap**
Scientific Name: *Cystoderma carcharias*
Size: Cap 1–10 cm, stem 3–9 cm
Distribution: Europe, Asia, Subantarctic Islands
Edibility: Inedible

Page: 130
Common Name: **Persistent Waxcap**
Scientific Name: *Hygrocybe acutoconica*
Size: Cap 3–6 cm, stem 9 cm
Distribution: North America, Europe
Edibility: Inedible

Page: 72
Common Name: **Pie Goat**
Scientific Name: *Scutiger pes-caprae* syn *Albatrellus pes-caprae*
Size: Cap 6–10 cm, stem 3–6 cm
Distribution: Europe
Edibility: Edible

Page: 93
Common Name: **Pig's Ear**
Scientific Name: *Gomphus clavatus*
Size: 4–10 cm wide, 2–7 cm tall
Distribution: Temperate and Subtropical Regions
Edibility: Edible

Page: 18–19
Common Name: **Piggyback Rosegill**
Scientific Name: *Volvariella surrecta*
Size: Cap 3–8 cm, stem 3–6 cm
Distribution: Europe, North Africa, North America, New Zealand. Rare.
Edibility: Suspect, easily confused with deadly *Amanita* fungi such as Deathcap and Destroying Angel

Page: 146
Common Name: **Plain Earthtongue**
Scientific Name: *Geoglossum umbratile*
Size: 3–10 cm
Distribution: Worldwide
Edibility: Edibility unknown

Page: 140
Common Name: **Plums and Custard**
Scientific Name: *Tricholomopsis rutilans*
Size: Cap 4–12 cm stem, 4–10 cm
Distribution: North America, Europe
Edibility: Inedible

Page: 12–13
Common Name: **Poplar Bells**
Scientific Name: *Schizophyllum amplum*
Size: Less than 5 cm wide
Distribution: Worldwide
Edibility: Inedible

Page: 144
Common Name: **Porcelain Fungus, Poached Egg Fungus**
Scientific Name: *Oudemansiella mucida*
Size: Cap 2–8 cm, stem 3–10 cm
Distribution: Europe
Edibility: Suspect. Edible after cleaning

Page: 94
Common Name: None
Scientific Name: *Pseudoaleuria fibrillosa*
Size: Less than 2 cm
Distribution: North America, Europe
Edibility: Edibility unknown

Page: 186
Common Name: **Rayed Earthstar**
Scientific Name: *Geastrum quadrifidum*
Size: Less than 5 cm
Distribution: The Americas, Europe, Africa, Asia, Australasia
Edibility: Inedible

Page: 33
Common Name: **Red Banded Webcap**
Scientific Name: *Cortinarius armillatus*
Size: Cap 4–12, stem 6–15 cm
Distribution: Europe, North America
Edibility: Poisonous/suspect, easily confused with other deadly webcap fungi

Page: 162–163
Common Name: **Red-Belt Conk**
Scientific Name: *Fomitopsis pinicola*
Size: Over 15 cm
Distribution: North America, Europe
Edibility: Inedible

Page: 139
Common Name: **Red-Tinted Russula**
Scientific Name: *Russula paludosa*
Size: Cap 5–15 cm, stem 4–15 cm
Distribution: North America, Europe
Edibility: Edible, but easily mistaken for poisonous *Russula emetic*

Page: 108–109
Common Name: **Rosy Goblet**
Scientific Name: *Microstoma protracta*
Size: Less than 5 cm
Distribution: North America, Europe
Edibility: Toxicity unknown

Page: 21
Common Name: **Royal Fly Agaric**
Scientific Name: *Amanita regalis*
Size: Cap over 15 cm, stem 15–25 cm
Distribution: Europe, North America.
Edibility: Poisonous/suspect, easily mistaken for the deadly *Aminata muscaria*

Page: 56–57
Common Name: **Russet Toughshank**
Scientific Name: *Gymnopus dryophilus*
Size: Cap 2–5 cm, stem 2–5 cm
Distribution: North America, Europe
Edibility: Edible

Page: 106–107
Common Name: **Sand Cup**
Scientific Name: *Geopora arenicola*
Size: Up to 2.5 cm tall, 1–2.5 cm wide
Distribution: North America, Europe
Edibility: Poisonous

Page: 137
Common Name: **Scarlet Elf Cup**
Scientific Name: *Sarcoscypha jurana*
Size: 1–5 cm
Distribution: North America, Europe
Edibility: Inedible

Page: 40
Common Name: **Shaggy Parasol**
Scientific Name: *Chlorophyllum rhacodes*
Size: Cap 5–15 cm, stem 5–20 cm
Distribution: Europe, North America
Edibility: Inedible/suspect

Page: 7, 38
Common Name: **Shaggy Scalycap**
Scientific Name: *Pholiota squarrosa*
Size: Cap 3–12 cm, stem 5–15 cm
Distribution: North America, Europe
Edibility: Inedible

Page: 138
Common Name: **The Sickener**
Scientific Name: *Russula emetica*
Size: Cap 3–10 cm, stem 4–9 cm
Distribution: North America, Europe
Edibility: Poisonous, easily mistaken for the edible *Russula paludosa*

Page: 34–35
Common Name: **Slimy Spike**
Scientific Name: *Gomphidius glutinosus*
Size: Cap 5–12 cm, stem 3.5–10 cm
Distribution: North America, Europe
Edibility: Inedible

Page: 132
Common Name: **Small Staghorn Fungus**
Scientific Name: *Calocera cornea*
Size: 2–12 mm tall, 1–2 mm wide
Distribution: North America, Europe
Edibility: Inedible

Page: 170–171
Common Name: **Snaketongue Truffleclub**
Scientific Name: *Cordyceps ophioglossoides*
Size: Less than 5 cm
Distribution: North America, Europe
Edibility: Inedible

Page: 133
Common Name: **Spectacular Rustgill**
Scientific Name: *Gymnopilus spectabilis* syn
Gymnopilus junonius
Size: Cap 4–20 cm, stem 5–12
Distribution: North America, Europe, Asia, Australia
Edibility: Poisonous, easily mistaken for several edible and deadly mushrooms

Page: 45
Common Name: **Spiny Puffball, Spring Puffball**
Scientific Name: *Lycoperdon echinatum*
Size: Fruitbody 1–5 cm wide, 3–7 cm tall
Distribution: Europe, North America
Edibility: Inedible

Page: 75
Common Name: **Split Porecrust**
Scientific Name: *Schizopora paradoxa*
Size: Spread 1–5 mm
Distribution: Europe
Edibility: Inedible

Page: 160
Common Name: **Splitgill, Common Porecrust**
Scientific Name: *Schizophyllum commune*
Size: Up to 4 cm
Distribution: Worldwide
Edibility: Inedible

Page: 164
Common Name: **Split Gill Fungus**
Scientific Name: *Schizophyllum amplum*
Size: 1–3 cm
Distribution: North America, Europe
Edibility: Inedible

Page: 113
Common Name: **Spring Hazel Cup**
Scientific Name: *Encoelia furfuracea*
Size: Up to 1.5 cm wide
Distribution: North America, Europe
Edibility: Inedible

Page: 73
Common Name: **Spring Polypore**
Scientific Name: *Polyporus arcularius*
Size: Cap 1–8 cm, stem 2–6 cm
Distribution: North America, Europe
Edibility: Inedible

Page: 82–83
Common Name: **Spruce Tooth**
Scientific Name: *Bankera violascens*
Size: Cap 3–13 cm, stem 3–10 cm
Distribution: North America, Europe
Edibility: Inedible

Page: 120–121
Common Name: **Stag's Horn**
Scientific Name: *Xylaria hypoxylon*
Size: 3–8 cm
Distribution: North America, Europe
Edibility: Inedible

Page: 118
Common Name: **Stinking Earthfan**
Scientific Name: *Thelephora palmata*
Size: Less than 10 cm
Distribution: North America, Europe, Asia, Australia, South America
Edibility: Inedible

Page: 150
Common Name: **Stump Fairy Helmet**
Scientific Name: *Mycena stipata*
Size: Cap 0.5–3 cm, stem 4–7 cm
Distribution: North America, Europe
Edibility: Inedible

Page: 152
Common Name: **Summer Bolete**
Scientific Name: *Bolbitius reticulatus*
Size: Cap 3–6 cm, stem 5–6 cm
Distribution: North America, Europe
Edibility: Poisonous/suspect

Page: 64
Common Name: **Tawny Funnel Cap**
Scientific Name: *Lepista flaccid*
Size: Cap 5–10 cm, stem 3–5 cm
Distribution: North America, Europe
Edibility: Inedible

Page: 16–17
Common Name: **Tawny Grisette**
Scientific Name: *Aminata fulva*
Size: Cap 4–9 cm, stem 7–15 cm
Distribution: North America, Europe
Edibility: Suspect, easily mistaken for deadly *Amanita* fungi such as Deathcap and Destroying Angel

Page: 81
Common Name: **Terracotta Hedgehog**
Scientific Name: *Hydnum rufescens*
Size: Cap 2–6 cm, stem 2–4 cm
Distribution: Europe
Edibility: Edible

Page: 41
Common Name: **Toothed Powdercap**
Scientific Name: *Flammulaster muricatus*
Size: Cap 1.5–3 cm, stem less than 5 cm
Distribution: Europe, North America
Edibility: Inedible

Page: 90–91
Common Name: **Trumpet Chanterelle**
Scientific Name: *Craterellus tubaeformis*
Size: Cap 2–5 cm, stem 5–8 cm
Distribution: North America, Europe
Edibility: Edible

Page: 44
Common Name: **Umber-brown Puffball**
Scientific Name: *Lycoperdon umbrinum*
Size: Fruitbody 2–3 cm wide, 2–4 cm tall
Distribution: China, Europe, North America
Edibility: Inedible/suspect.

Page: 66–67
Common Name: **Velvet Rollrim**
Scientific Name: *Tapinella atrotomentosa*
Size: Funnel 10–30 cm, stem 3–8 cm
Distribution: Worldwide
Edibility: Inedible

Page: 60–61
Common Name: **Velvet Shank**
Scientific Name: *Flammulina velutipes*
Size: Cap 1–20 cm, stem 2–11 cm
Distribution: North America, Europe, cultivated in Asia
Edibility: Edible

Page: 58
Common Name: **Velvety Milk Cap**
Scientific Name: *Lactarius lignyotus*
Size: Cap 2–9 cm, stem 4–10 cm
Distribution: North America
Edibility: Inedible

Page: 141
Common Name: **Verdigris Roundhead**
Scientific Name: *Stropharia aeruginosa*
Size: Cap 2.5–8 cm, stem 2–6 cm
Distribution: North America, Europe
Edibility: Poisonous

Page: 143
Common Name: **Violet Webcap**
Scientific Name: *Cortinarius violaceus*
Size: Cap 4–15 cm, stem 6–12 cm
Distribution: Europe, the Americas, Asia, New Zealand, Australia
Edibility: Poisonous/suspect, easily confused with edible *Lepita nuda*. Avoid all *Cortinarius* fungi

Page: 150–151
Common Name: **Winter Bonnet**
Scientific Name: *Mycena tintinnabulum*
Size: Cap 0.5–3 cm, stem 1–5 cm
Distribution: Europe. Rare.
Edibility: Inedible

Page: 142–143
Common Name: **Wood Blewit**
Scientific Name: *Lepista nuda*
Size: Cap 6–15 cm, stem, 5–10 cm
Distribution: North America, Europe
Edibility: Edible/suspect. Must be thoroughly cooked. Easily confused with the many poisonous *Cortinarius* fungi

Page: 110
Common Name: **Cauliflower**
Scientific Name: *Sparassis crispa*
Size: 20–50 cm tall, 40 cm wide
Distribution: North America, Europe
Edibility: Edible

Page: 78–79
Common Name: **Wood Hedgehog**
Scientific Name: *Hydnum repandum*
Size: Cap 4–15 cm, stem 4–10 cm
Distribution: North America, Europe, Australia, Asia. Rare.
Edibility: Edible

Page: 190–191
Common Name: **Weather Earthstar**
Scientific Name: *Geastrum corollinum*
Size: Less than 5 cm
Distribution: Europe
Edibility: Inedible

Page: 131
Common Name: **Yellow Brain Fungus, Witch's Butter**
Scientific Name: *Tremella mesenterica*
Size: 2–8 cm
Distribution: Temperate and tropical regions
Edibility: Inedible/suspect

Page: 153
Common Name: **Yellow Fieldcap**
Scientific Name: *Bolbitius titubans*
Size: Cap 1–4 cm, stem 3–12 cm
Distribution: North America, Europe
Edibility: Inedible